BIG MACHINES FOR BIG JOBS

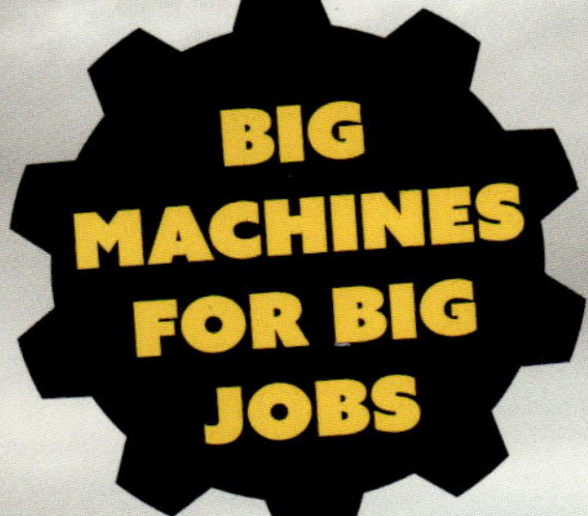

TRACTORS ON THE JOB

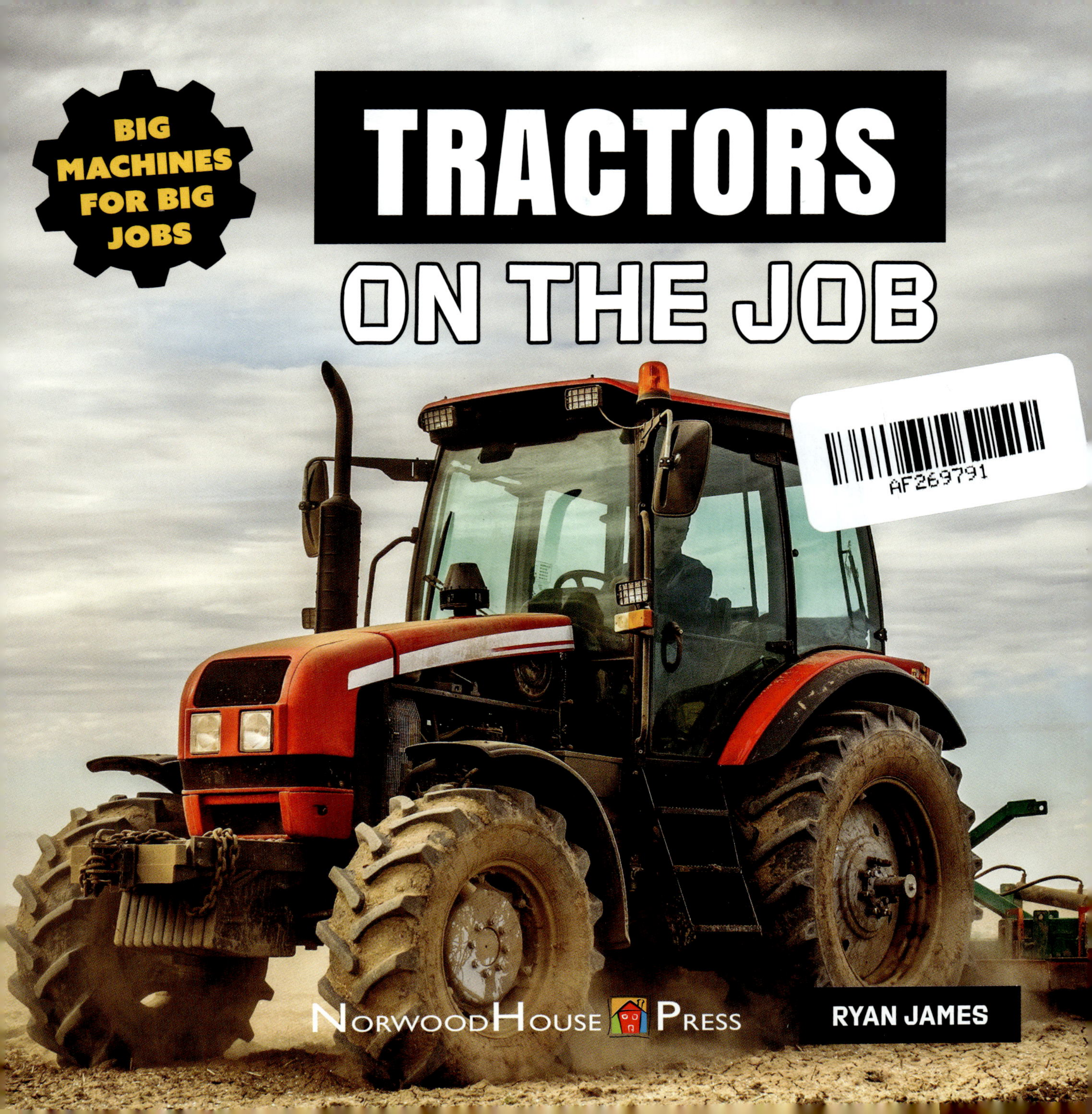

NORWOOD HOUSE PRESS

RYAN JAMES

Cataloging-in-Publication Data

Names: James, Ryan.
Title: Tractors on the job / Ryan James.
Description: Buffalo, NY : Norwood House Press, 2026. | Series: Big machines for big jobs | Includes glossary and index.
Identifiers: ISBN 9781978573963 (pbk.) | ISBN 9781978573970 (library bound) | ISBN 9781978573987 (ebook)
Subjects: LCSH: Tractors--Juvenile literature.
Classification: LCC TL233.15 J359 2026 | DDC 631.3'72--dc23

Published in 2026 by
Norwood House Press
2544 Clinton Street
Buffalo, NY 14224

Copyright © 2026 Norwood House Press
Designer: Rhea Magaro
Editor: Kim Thompson

Photo credits: Cover, pp. 1, 3 oticki/Shutterstock.com; p. 5 MAVV/Shutterstock.com; p. 6 BG Media/Shutterstock.com; p. 7 Sheryl Watson/Shutterstock.com; p. 9 Saeedatun/Shutterstock.com; p. 10 Galdric PS/Shutterstock.com; p. 11 Adwo/Shutterstock.com; p. 12 Maksim Safaniuk/Shutterstock.com; p. 13 Gerard Koudenburg/Shutterstock.com; p. 14 F01 PHOTO/Shutterstock.com; p. 17 PeopleImages.com Yuri A/Shutterstock.com; p. 18 F Armstrong Photography/Shutterstock.com; p. 19 SergeyKlopotov/Shutterstock.com; p. 21 NewJadsada/Shutterstock.com;

Printed in the United States of America

Some of the images in this book illustrate individuals who are models. The depictions do not imply actual situations or events.

CPSIA compliance information: Batch #CSNHP26: For further information contact Norwood House Press at 1-800-237-9932.

Find us on 

TABLE OF CONTENTS

PARTS OF A TRACTOR

Tractors are big machines. Many tractors have four wheels.

The front of a tractor has a cab. The driver sits there. The tractor's **engine** is under the hood.

There is a **hitch** on the back of
a tractor.

WHAT DOES A TRACTOR DO?

A tractor works on a farm. The hitch attaches to different tools. The tractor pulls the tools around. A tractor can pull a **harvester** through **fields**.

A tractor's engine burns **gasoline**. The engine powers the tractor.

Is a tool hitched to the tractor? The tractor's engine can power it too!

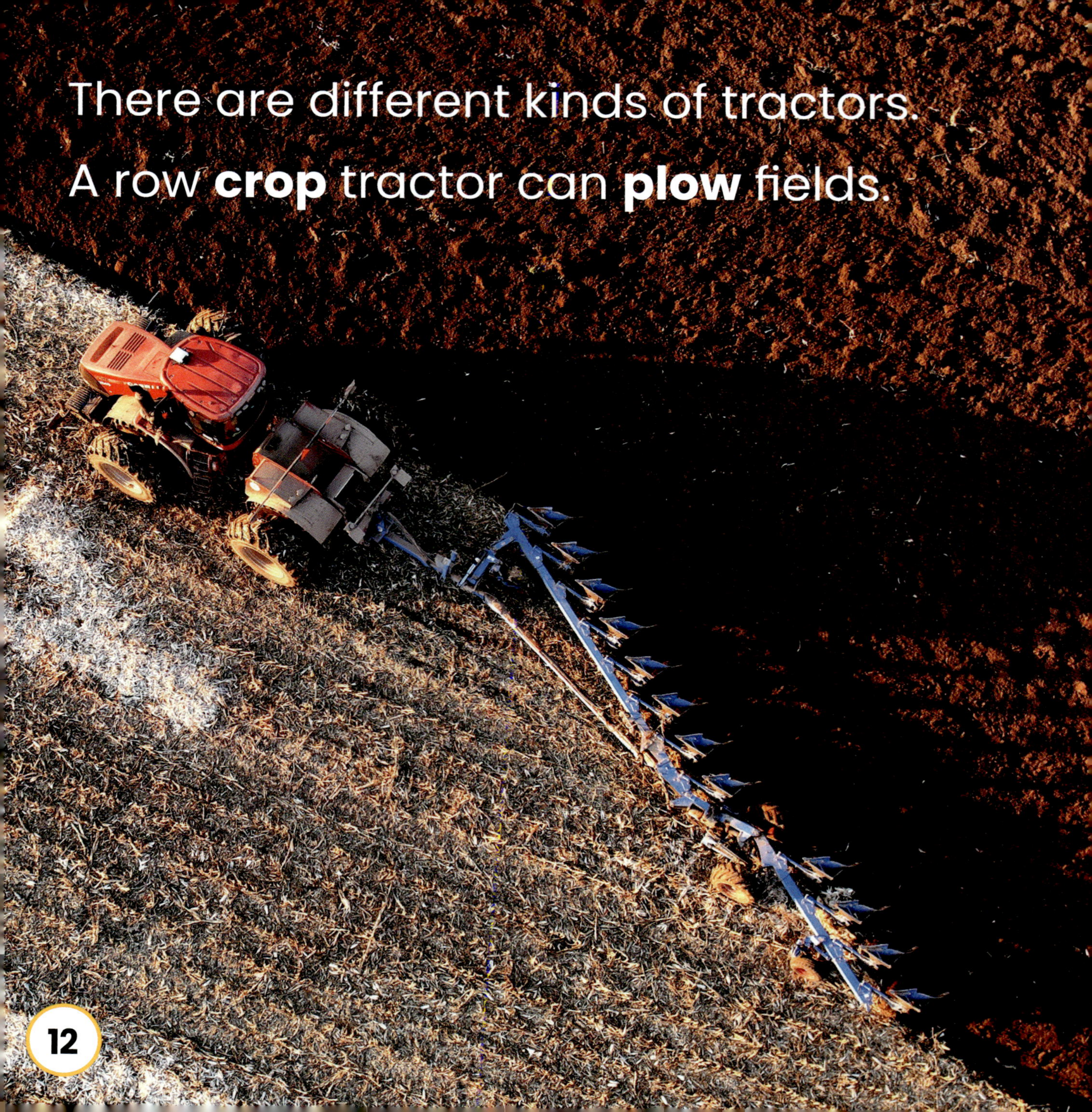

There are different kinds of tractors.
A row **crop** tractor can **plow** fields.

A utility tractor does big jobs. It can haul **livestock**.

Garden tractors are used in yards.
They mow lawns. They clear snow.

TRACTOR SAFETY

Stay safe around tractors so nobody gets hurt. An adult should always be with you.

When a tractor is working, stay out of its path. This lets the tractor keep going.

Do not touch tools hitched to a tractor. Some have sharp **blades** that could hurt you.

TRACTORS IN ACTION

Tractors are **vehicles** on the job. They get all kinds of work done on the farm!

GLOSSARY

blades (blades): flat, sharp-edged tools for cutting

crop (krahp): a plant grown on a farm for food

engine (EN-jin): the part of a machine that makes it run

fields (feeldz): pieces of open land used for growing crops on a farm

gasoline (GAS-uh-leen): a liquid engine fuel made from oil

harvester (HAHR-vi-stur): a machine that gathers crops from fields

hitch (hich): a device that connects tools and machines to the tractor

livestock (LIVE-stahk): animals raised on farms, such as cows and chickens

plow (plou): to break up soil and get it ready for planting

vehicles (VEE-i-kuhlz): machines used to move people or things from one place to another

THINKING QUESTIONS

1. What is the job of a tractor?

2. How is each type of tractor different from the others?

3. Where do tractors work?

4. How can you stay safe around a tractor?

5. Why are tractors important?

INDEX

ABOUT THE AUTHOR

Ryan James lives in the mountains of North Carolina where he goes hiking with his dog Bailey. He loves fly fishing, visiting farms in the area, and picking fresh produce. He has always enjoyed writing and wrote his first book as a teenager.